CORNWALL'S RAIL

Tony F
Revised by

Tor Mark • Redruth

The Tor Mark series

This third edition first published 2002 by Tor Mark,
PO Box 4, Redruth, Cornwall TR16 5YX

Reprinted 2003.

© 1990, 2002 Tor Mark

ISBN 0-85025-394-2

Acknowledgements
The photographs are reproduced by kind permission as follows: Tony Fairclough
Collection pages 6, 22 and 48b; Mrs Audrey Mills page 9; Bernard Mills cover and
pages 18, 23, 26, 38, 41, 44, 45, 46 and 48a; Royal Institution of Cornwall pages 1, 11,
12, 14, 15, 28, 31, 34, 36. Other photographs from the publishers' own collection.

Printed in Great Britain by R Booth (Troutbeck Press), Mabe, Cornwall

THE POLDICE-PORTREATH TRAMROAD

In Cornwall at the beginning of the nineteenth century, few people travelled outside their immediate environment, unless they were obliged to do so. Transport was confined to either horse-drawn vehicle or sailing ship. Tourism was as yet something in the distant future.

Most early Cornish railways came into being because of local development. With the boom years of tin and copper mining, it became virtually impossible to cope with the conveyance of ore to the coast by pack horses and also with the large quantities of coal to be brought inland from the ships to supply the mine pumping engines. Later, after years of faithful service, these mineral railways were doomed to die when the industry ceased to function.

The first of these lines was the Poldice to Portreath tramroad, constructed to link the harbour at Portreath on the north coast with various copper mines around Scorrier and St Day. It was built at the instigation of mine owners and merchants of the area, who themselves remained the sole users of the line. The Company had complete control not only of the tramroad but also of the port. The first rail was laid at Portreath by Lord de Dunstanville on 25 October 1809 and the line from Portreath harbour as far as Scorrier House was in use by September 1812. The section from Scorrier to Poldice was undertaken in 1818 and the whole line opened early the following year. Together with a branch to Treskerby it cost about £20,000 and was of approximately 4 ft gauge being horse worked throughout. It was constructed as a plate-way, using flanged L-shaped cast iron plates on square granite blocks. Poldice was in those days an important and productive copper mine but by 1856 it was practically exhausted. Symons' *Gazetteer of Cornwall* (1884) quotes the tramroad as being 'much in use till the stoppage of Poldice in the sixties'. He recalls that in 1830 he rode in one of the cars to a tea-party, though there was no provision for the conveyance of passengers. Although the tramway also served other mines, it was little used by 1865 and closed completely soon after, the tramplates being taken up and sold for scrap around 1882.

THE REDRUTH & CHASEWATER RAILWAY

The important Redruth & Chasewater Railway was purely mineral, serving the rich copper area of Gwennap, and had the distinction of remaining completely independent during its lifetime. In 1820 the fortunes of the Gwennap mines were increasing rapidly, the most important being Consols and United Mines, and the horses used to convey the large quantities of copper ore to the coast found it increasingly difficult on poor tracks.

A railway was authorised on 17 June 1824 with a capital of £22,500. Of 4 ft gauge it had wrought iron rails set in cast-iron chairs bolted to granite blocks and, for the first time in Cornwall, edge rails were used. It was single track with several passing loops. There was an official opening on 30 January 1826, when some of the proprietors travelled in three covered wagons from Wheal Buller to Narabo quays, near present day Devoran. The downward journey was made by gravity and the return journey with the assistance of a horse. It is probable that wagons were in use the previous year on some sections of the line as they were completed. The Company were not carriers in their own right, but had powers to levy tolls for the traffic they carried. In November 1826 the line was completed from Narabo quays into Devoran itself, and the following year saw the completion of the sections from Wheal Buller northwards to Redruth and from Devoran to Point quay.

Vast quantities of copper ore were transported to Devoran for shipment to South Wales and increasing amounts of coal, imported by the same vessels, were brought up the line to serve the ever-deepening mines. Traffic was well in excess of 60,000 tons annually in the 1830s and the Company made annual profits approaching £3000. The great Consols and United Mines each had long branches and storage sidings and some indication of their magnitude is seen in that in one year they used 15,000 tons of coal. By the end of that decade the Hayle Railway had reached Redruth and a branch from it actually crossed the Redruth & Chasewater.

The man responsible for the success of the railway was its General Manager, John Taylor, who was also Manager of a number of the mines in the area, including both Consols and United Mines in their heyday. In 1847 the railway company bought a steam tug, *Sydney*, to be used for towing vessels in and out of Devoran. The vessel had a useful life but one beset by mishaps and difficulties.

Up to 1854 the wagons had been worked by horses, but in November of that year the Company took delivery of two tank engines, *Miner* and

Smelter. They were odd looking machines with square tanks, tall chimneys and without cabs, and ran between Devoran and Ting Tang, above Carharrack where there was an interchange point. From here the wagons were pulled by the Company's own horses, bought to avoid the use of outside carriers. Eventually the locomotives worked the whole length from Devoran to Wheal Buller near Redruth. In September 1859 it was necessary to acquire a third locomotive, *Spitfire,* much improved but similar in appearance to its predecessors, for traffic was by then around 90,000 tons annually. The Company's headquarters were at Devoran and there they built workshops to repair and maintain the locomotives and wagons. *Miner* was largely rebuilt in 1869 at these very works. At Devoran the wagons ran at a level 10 ft above the storage area for ore so as to facilitate unloading. A guard and two brakesmen travelled on the wagons, which were uncoupled by the brakesmen operating from the square wooden buffer-blocks. Miners and other unofficial passengers also used this dangerous mode of travel. The guard used white, green and red flags or a code of arm signals to the driver; according to the Rule Book it was permissible to signal 'Danger!' by violently waving a hat.

Gradually traffic decreased with the closure of the copper mines in the locality and in 1879 a Receiver was appointed, although the line continued to function for a further 36 years. *Smelter* was kept mostly in reserve, and with the track in a poor state, derailments were not infrequent. The branch to Chacewater, although started in 1853, was never completed. The end came on 25 September 1915, when the ever faithful *Miner,* still well kept and in reasonable running order, took the last train down to Devoran, whose working life as a port had virtually ended. It was perhaps appropriate that *Miner,* currently in steam and by far the most reliable of the locomotives, should work the last train.

THE PENTEWAN RAILWAY

The Pentewan Railway was constructed to facilitate the transport of china clay from the fast growing areas close to St Austell to the harbour at Pentewan. Although parliamentary powers were not obtained, Sir Christopher Hawkins, who was also responsible for building the harbour, constructed the railway. Only four miles long, it was built to the unusual gauge of 2 ft 6 in and was opened in the summer of 1829.

Canopus taking a Sunday School outing to Pentewan

Clay was laboriously carried by horses to the railway depot off West Hill, St Austell, whence the wagons were conveyed by gravity. They came to rest on the level along the line and finished the remainder horse-pulled. Pentewan quickly overhauled nearby Charlestown in outgoing traffic and in those early years about one third of the clay produced in the county was shipped via Pentewan, though this dropped to about one tenth in subsequent years. In 1889 for example the total traffic carried was 45,000 tons. Throughout its lifetime, the Pentewan Railway suffered from recurrent silting of the harbour due to sediment precipitated by clay waste brought down the river; efforts were made to sweep it away by opening large reservoirs specially built for the purpose. There was also considerable flooding of the lower end of the line and through lack of resources the track was not maintained in a good condition.

The line received belated official recognition by the incorporation of the Pentewan Railway & Harbour Co Ltd in February 1873. It was not until the following year that the introduction of locomotives was authorised. The first engine was named *Pentewan* but this had to be replaced by a similar one, *Trewithen*, in 1886. *Trewithen* was itself replaced by

Canopus in 1901, whilst *Pioneer* was bought second-hand in 1912 to supplement it. The engines ran only as far as Iron Bridge, and the uppermost section into St Austell was horse worked in the interests of public safety; the horses were brought up on the first train of the day from Pentewan. In later years however the engines were able to run over the whole length.

One 16 seat saloon carriage was built in 1875, but its use was confined solely to the Hawkins family. Although there was no official passenger service, passengers were conveyed soon after the line opened. An early account quotes the fare as three pence. From the 1880s onwards, annual Sunday School parties were carried free to Pentewan in the clay wagons. At St Austell there were a number of sidings and a clay storage shed whilst sidings at London Apprentice served the village and mine at Polgooth. At Pentewan there were four branches, as well as warehouses, a clay storage shed and an engine shed. One branch ran on to a wooden structure, some 5 ft high alongside the dock to facilitate unloading. Apart from china clay and china stone, outgoing traffic included some iron ore and tin, whilst coal, limestone and sand were conveyed inwards.

The decline of the line was due to poor harbour facilities compared with the growing importance of Par and Fowey, plus its inability, through lack of funds, to extend further into the clay territory. The Goonbarrow branch on the Cornwall Minerals Railway, opened in 1893, took much of their potential and the Pentewan Railway remained in isolation, never reaching the Cornwall Railway's main line. The last freight was conveyed on 2 March 1918 and shortly afterwards the rails were lifted.

THE BODMIN & WADEBRIDGE RAILWAY

In 1831 Sir William Molesworth, a prominent landowner, engaged Roger Hopkins to make a survey for a railway from Wadebridge to Wenford Bridge, with branches from Dunmere and Grogley to Ruthern Bridge. The initial purpose of this was to convey sea sand from Wadebridge to the farmlands of the fertile Camel valley, unlike most early Cornish railways whose object was to convey ore or china clay to the coast for shipment. With a capital of £22,500 the Bodmin & Wadebridge Railway received its assent on 23 May 1832, considerable expense being saved by Sir William giving land to the Company. Substantially built on granite blocks, it was the first standard, sometimes called narrow gauge railway in Cornwall. Stone posts were placed at quarter mile intervals, in advance of the legal requirement to do so, and others were placed at Wenford Bridge, Bodmin and Ruthern Bridge, showing the exact distance from the Company's headquarters at Wadebridge.

Although the Company had only one engine at the outset, *Camel*, it could boast of being the first locomotive line in Cornwall. It was opened from Wadebridge to Dunmere Junction and from there to Bodmin on 4 July 1834 followed by the remainder from Dunmere to Wenford Bridge, and Grogley to Ruthern Bridge on 30 September. On this day a special train carried passengers free, first to Wenford Bridge and then to Bodmin. A special constable was placed in each carriage. Cheap day tickets were issued from the outset and excursions were run to cattle markets, flower shows, swimming matches, bazaars and the like. On one day in 1836 for example, some 800 people went from Wadebridge to Wenford Bridge on an excursion at one shilling each. On the Wenford Bridge and Ruthern Bridge sections, passengers were also carried unofficially in the tool wagon. A special excursion was even run to Bodmin in 1840 to enable passengers to witness the public execution of the Lightfoot brothers.

In those early days there was a service from Wadebridge to Bodmin and back twice a week, with goods services on remaining days. A second engine, *Elephant*, was bought in 1836. When *Camel* was out of commission, horses had to be used and on one occasion the engine herself was hauled by horses after a breakdown. Trains would stop anywhere to load or unload, but if a load so delivered was not removed in one hour a fine was imposed. On one occasion a train stopped to allow a man to retrieve his purse. Coaches were built in the Company's own workshops; two early examples, one closed second class, the other open third class, withdrawn from service in 1887, are now preserved at the York Railway Museum. At Wadebridge the line extended to the quay alongside the river and a sand dock was in use. The original engine shed and workshops survived until 1969. Wharves or depots, some of which had female wharfingers, were situated at Ruthern Bridge, Nanstallon, Dunmere, Bodmin, Helland, Tresarrett and Wenford Bridge.

Steam on the preserved Bodmin & Wenford Bridge Railway, at Colesloggett Woods in December 1999. In fine form, 'Ugly' powers a Santa Special up the grade

At Wenford Bridge the line was linked by an incline built in the 1890s to the De Lank granite quarries. The Company also built the road and bridge leading to Nanstallon village and was responsible for planting avenues of elm trees to cover the route.

The first Superintendent was named Dunstan. He was succeeded by Hays Kyd, noted for his famous cocoa tickets and sometimes ale, authorised to the staff in lieu of overtime, which was at the rate of sixpence an hour. Kyd retired in 1888 with a pension of £250 a year.

In 1846 the London & South Western Railway, to keep the Cornwall Railway at bay, bought the Bodmin & Wadebridge, although at the time this isolated line was 200 miles from the parent railway's system. It was not until forty years later, in 1886, that an Act of Parliament legalised the acquisition. In the early years Ruthern Bridge and Nanstallon produced a variety of minerals whilst further ore and considerable quantities of granite were conveyed from Wenford Bridge. China clay traffic started in 1862 and was to become the mainstay of the Wenford line and the reason for its continued existence. In the 1870s attempts were made to extend from Wenford Bridge to Delabole and from Ruthern Bridge to the Cornwall Minerals Railway, but these proved abortive. Shooting Range Platform, a halt near Wadebridge, was built in the 1880s to serve a nearby rifle range.

The Great Western Railway opened the line from Bodmin Road (now Bodmin Parkway) to Bodmin in May 1887 with the customary public ceremony at Bodmin Station, and in September 1888 extended to Boscarne Junction on the Bodmin & Wadebridge. The latter improved their line by replacing granite sleepers to enable GWR trains to use it. Deviations were required near Grogley and Dunmere Junction. It had taken 54 years for the Bodmin and Wadebridge to be connected to a main line, and even then not the line of its owners. Trains from Bodmin Road had to reverse at Bodmin before proceeding to Wadebridge.

Agreement was reached to control the GWR's running rights to Wadebridge, where a new station was built. In this the GWR and LSWR maintained their own inspectors and ticket offices, a situation which continued until 1915. LSWR passenger services had to be suspended from 1887 for reconstruction and the service was not resumed until 1 November 1895. On the preceding 1 June, the LSWR's North Cornwall line had been opened to Wadebridge, at last connecting the Bodmin & Wadebridge with the system of its owners.

In 1906 halts were opened at Grogley, Nanstallon and Dunmere and steam rail motor cars introduced. No lights were provided at Grogley so the motor car did not stop there after dark! St Lawrence Platform, between Bodmin and Boscarne, constructed in 1906, was in use only until 1917. Sand traffic finished around 1920 and, with the closure of the mines, the Ruthern Bridge branch ceased on New Year's Day 1934.

Beattie well tank engines arrived in Wadebridge in 1893 and per-formed yeoman service, especially on the difficult Wenford Bridge branch, where they operated until 1962. Until 1964 steam trains used the water tank at Penhargard in Pencarrow Woods, fed by gravity from an adjoining stream. Subsequently the line was operated by a diesel shunter, conveying considerable quantities of china clay from Stannon on the edge of Bodmin Moor via Boscarne Junction to the main line at Bodmin Road. Closure came on 21 November 1983, just before the 150th anniversary.

Redruth Station c1863, when it was in the hands of the West Cornwall Railway, and before dual gauge track was introduced in 1866

THE HAYLE RAILWAY

The Hayle Railway covered an area from Redruth and Portreath westward to Hayle. The growing importance of Hayle as a mining port led to the incorporation of the Hayle Railway Company by an Act of 27 June 1834. At that time packhorses carrying ore converged on the port in large numbers and the necessity for a railway became more and more evident, especially in view of the success of the Redruth & Chasewater. The foundry at Hayle was expanding and at nearby Copperhouse there was a large smelting works.

With a capital of £64,000 the line was opened in stages from December 1837, from Hayle Foundry to Roskear and North Crofty. The following year saw the opening of the section from Portreath Junction on to Redruth and from Redruth Junction to Tresavean, some 17 miles in all.

Locomotives were used from the outset on most of the system, a distinct advantage over the Redruth & Chasewater whose traffic was horse-drawn at this time. The exceptions were at Hayle and Portreath

Redruth Station, 1 March 1867, with the first broad gauge train from Penzance, pulled by the South Devon Railway's 4-4-0 ST Lance

and the adjacent inclines. Horses operated from the lower end of Angarrack Incline into Hayle but by 1843 the engines were allowed to negotiate Angarrack, attached to the ropes of the incline, and therefore could run into Hayle. Further inclines were situated at Penponds, west of Camborne, about half a mile in length and operated on the counterbalance principle, and at Tresavean. Standard gauge was adopted and the track was single line, except on the inclines. The Company had a central depot at Pool, later to become Carn Brea, and usually employed five locomotives. *Cornubia*, one of the locomotives later taken over by the West Cornwall in 1846, was built at Copperhouse Foundry in 1838, probably the first locomotive to be made in Cornwall.

Passengers had sometimes travelled in the open mineral wagons, but the first passenger service between Hayle and Redruth took place on 22 May 1843, when about 200 people travelled free in two passenger carriages and three wagons, the carriages or 'omnibuses' as they were called, provided by Will Crotch of Hayle. A contemporary report read: 'On Monday last this line of railway was opened for the conveyance of passengers and, as no charge was made for that day, the carriages were literally crammed with persons of both sexes, who were anxious to enjoy the luxury of a gratuitous ride. We are glad to learn that although the train went three times over the line during the day, no accident of any consequence occurred.' The first passenger trains were in fact 'mixed trains', coaches being attached to the rear of the goods wagons. Some accidents occurred on Angarrack and other inclines. One notable example happened in 1844, involving the rear section of a train from Hayle, which was being hauled up the Angarrack incline, when the wire rope broke. The runaway portion increased speed rapidly and ended quite safely back at Hayle but some passengers who had jumped out were injured.

Stations were situated at Hayle, Copperhouse, Angarrack, Gwinear, Penponds, Camborne, Pool and Redruth. Excursion trains soon followed and Sunday School outings were especially popular. Moreover the public could use a regular horse-drawn omnibus from Redruth to reach Truro or Falmouth, or from Hayle to reach Penzance. The Portreath branch carried large quantities of ore for smelting, exchanged from the main line at Carn Brea Yard, and on the return journey coal from South Wales unloaded at the harbour for the steam engines at the mines. The extensive sidings were kept continually busy, as was the lengthy rope-worked incline. This was of double track and worked by a stationary locomotive used as the winding engine.

The line to Tresavean from Redruth Junction provided an important link with the extensive mining area around Gwennap, and although it crossed the Redruth & Chasewater Railway no exchange of traffic took place. The half-mile-long incline was also rope-worked, but in this instance by counter-balance. The engine proceeded up the incline first, and then the coal trucks ascended, at the same time as the wagons of ore descended. Both the Portreath and Tresavean lines closed in 1936. Near Camborne, sidings served the tin mines at Crofty and Roskear and the mighty Dolcoath copper mine.

Nº 12 Redruth *at Carn Brea, where it was built for the WCR in January 1864*

THE WEST CORNWALL RAILWAY

With a view to reconstructing the Hayle Railway and extending it from Redruth to Truro and from Hayle to Penzance, the West Cornwall was authorised on 3 August 1846 with capital of £500,000.

The new company took possession of the Hayle Railway on 3 November 1846 and intended using the broad gauge of 7 ft $0^{1}/_{4}$ in employed by the Cornwall Railway. However they later obtained permission to retain the narrower gauge, provided the track was made wide enough subsequently to accommodate the broad gauge. Brunel decided to use a new type of rail, known as Barlow rail, which was laid directly and deeply into the ballast. This was to cause considerable trouble and a number of derailments, so that in years to follow it had to be replaced.

Early in 1852, the old Hayle Railway line was closed for reconstruction and conversion. The inclines at Penponds and Angarrack were

Penzance Station c1870. A new embankment was necessary in 1921 and the station was rebuilt in 1937 to cater for increased holiday traffic

by-passed by viaducts, and the new line left Hayle by a viaduct. Of the other viaducts, Penzance, 347 yards long, was subject to sea damage and had to be replaced in 1871, this time surviving until an embankment was built in 1921. Although comparatively light timber structures, the viaducts of the West Cornwall line typified Brunel's expert design. A passenger service between Redruth and Penzance commenced on 11 March 1852 with three trains run daily, and two on Sundays. All services took one hour to accomplish the $16^1/2$ miles. Single fares were 3s. first class, 2s. second class and 1s. 4d. third class. It was intended to install a lift from Hayle viaduct to the old station and sidings, but instead the Hayle Wharves branch was built and due to its steep gradient, possessed one of the first sand drags to catch runaway trains. By 25 August the extension from Redruth to Higher Town, above Truro, was opened.

In 1855 another extension was opened to Newham, close by Truro on the Fal, where there was a wharf. This became the Truro terminus until

A typical summer weekend scene in the early 1950s, with the 'Cornish Riviera Express' at St Ives, which like many other resorts was opened up to tourism by the railways

1859 when the Cornwall Railway linked Plymouth to Truro. After that date the main service ran from Penwithers Junction to the new Cornwall Railway station at Truro, and the Newham section became a branch. Intermediate stations between Truro and Penzance were: Chacewater, Scorrier Gate, Redruth, Pool, Camborne, Gwinear Road, Angarrack (closed in 1852), Hayle, St Ives Road and Marazion Road. The break of gauge at Truro caused considerable delay as well as inconvenience and in 1864 the Cornwall Railway insisted, as they had the right to do under an earlier Act, that broad gauge be laid from Truro westwards. The West Cornwall were not in a financial position to comply and the following year the Company was leased jointly to the Great Western, Bristol & Exeter and South Devon Railway Companies.

On 1 January 1866 they became the absolute owners, and as such were responsible for laying the broad gauge, although the narrow gauge was retained as well.

The first broad gauge goods train to Penzance ran on 6 November 1866 and the first broad gauge passenger train on 1 March 1867. Daily passenger services comprised four trains of broad gauge and one of narrow. Local goods traffic continued with narrow gauge whilst through freight trains used broad gauge. From 1871 freight trains with wagons of both gauges were run. At the outset the West Cornwall took over five locomotives from the pioneer Hayle Railway and of the later additions, several were built at their own workshops at Carn Brea, as were many of the wagons. The last West Cornwall locomotive in service was *Fox*, built for the company in 1872. It became No. 1391 when the GWR took possession of the rolling stock, and worked in Cornwall until 1897 when it was rebuilt, to continue elsewhere until 1948.

The St Ives branch was opened in June 12 1877 as part of the West Cornwall. This 4 1/2 mile line followed the coast from St Erth and had the distinction of being the last section of railway constructed for Brunel's broad gauge. Intermediate stations were situated at Lelant and Carbis Bay. In 1888 mixed gauge was provided as far as Lelant to permit standard gauge goods trains to reach the quay there.

In 1878 the WCR passed completely to the GWR, which absorbed both the Bristol & Exeter and South Devon Railways, though due to an oversight the WCR continued a nominal existence until 1948.

THE CORNWALL RAILWAY

In 1846 the Cornwall Railway had formulated plans to link Plymouth with Truro and Falmouth, together with several branches. Work commenced near Truro in August 1847 but in the following years very little progress was made, due largely to forfeiture of shares and subsequent lack of capital. By 1852 the Truro-Falmouth line was partly completed, but this was then left in abeyance to concentrate on the Plymouth-Truro section. The Cornwall Railway was leased to the Great Western, Bristol & Exeter and South Devon Railways jointly from 1861, having been partly financed and leased to them as early as 1855, and on its eventual opening was worked by a committee representing the three associated companies and the Cornwall Railway.

Brunel's Royal Albert Bridge in 1976

On 4 May 1859 the line from Plymouth Millbay over the Tamar and on to Truro was opened to the public, with cheering crowds and blaring brass bands at many stations to welcome the first train. The line was single track initially, with passing loops at nearly all the stations. Goods traffic commenced about five months later. Brunel, who had joined the GWR at the age of 27, lived long enough to see his triumph, the Royal Albert Bridge, completed. Over 700 yards long and containing 4000 tons of iron, it rose 100 ft above the Tamar and was probably the most spectacular of all his works. It cost £225,000 and was ceremonially opened by Prince Albert. A contemporary writer remarked that the bridge 'spanned the silver streak which separated the Briton from the Englishman', and the expansion of the railway system would destroy 'the isolation of the wild West'. Built to Brunel's famous broad gauge, which facilitated speeds far higher than elsewhere, it did however necessitate the interchange of traffic at Truro until in 1864 the Cornwall Railway insisted that an additional rail be laid for the wider gauge.

A feature of the Cornwall line is the large number of splendid viaducts, 34 between Plymouth and Truro, and covering some four miles in all. Brunel's every conception was on a colossal scale, but reductions in capital expenditure before the line was built led to urgent needs for economy and Brunel's grand ideas had constantly to be reduced in scale. Lofty viaducts, relatively cheap to build, traversed deep valleys. However, construction in this way greatly increased the future costs of maintenance. When built, these typical Brunel viaducts had tall masonry piers, 66ft apart, supporting spans of timber, again for reasons of economy. St Pinnock was 153ft high, with those at Liskeard and Moorswater nearby nearly as lofty, whilst the one at Truro was 443 yards long. Replacement of the timber spans by masonry structures or wrought iron truss girders began in 1871.

Stations at the opening were situated at Saltash, St Germans, Menheniot, Liskeard, Lostwithiel, Par, St Austell, Grampound Road and Truro. Bodmin Road was opened some weeks later, Doublebois the following year and Burngullow in 1863. In 1845 Brunel had said that the character of the country in Cornwall was such that it would only be possible to put a railway across it at moderate expense by 'sacrificing all consideration for the (convenience) of the population'. In order to avoid sharp curves and steep gradients and to maintain levels, Liskeard, St Austell and Truro stations all had to be built some distance from the town centres. The Company by-passed Bodmin, by building Bodmin Road, because it would have cost £11,000 more to go into Bodmin itself. It was not until thirty years later in 1887 that the branch was built. The delay in opening Bodmin Road was due to doubts as to whether it

College Wood Viaduct, Penryn, seen here in 1902, was the last of Brunel's wooden viaducts to be used for passenger traffic. It was replaced in 1934

should be situated there or just a short distance away at Respryn. where a private station was in use for Lanhydrock House. Respryn was open to public traffic for the few weeks until Bodmin Road was completed, and in use privately for several years. The single line to Falmouth was eventually opened on 24 August 1863. It followed a course to Penwithers Junction where it cut across the Newham branch. There were stations at Perran, Penryn and Falmouth. Early the following year Perran was renamed Perranwell and the connection to Falmouth Dock was opened. Penmere Platform in Falmouth was not opened until 1925. Among its eight viaducts, again the famous wooden structures, were Carnon, where the Redruth & Chasewater line passed at right angles beneath, Penryn and College Wood.

Passenger services on the Cornwall Railway altered little, with five trains each way on weekdays and two each way on Sundays. Until 1876 third class fares were a penny a mile, so that a single ticket from Plymouth to Truro cost 4s. 5½d. By comparison the second class fare was 7s.10d. and first class 11s. 6d. A serious accident occurred in 1873 when there was a head-on collision between a goods train and a mail train. This resulted from the signalman at Menheniot shouting 'Right away, Dick'. Unfortunately the guards on both goods trains at the station were called Richard and the wrong one acted on the instruction. Some months prior to this, the driver of a passenger train between Par and St Austell avoided a head-on crash when a runaway train of china clay came towards him. Showing great presence of mind he quickly reversed to safety. In its early days the drive to establish the Cornwall Railway and especially its extension to Falmouth was largely inspired by a belief in the growing prosperity and importance of Falmouth as a port. This was not to be, although ship repairing there has led to considerable goods traffic to the docks. Most of the mineral traffic continued to concentrate on the lines leading to the ports, and of these lines only the West Cornwall linked with the Cornwall Railway. In the 1870s the great mining depression set in, and it was not until after this time that tourism began to increase and so provide traffic for the main lines.

Although it provided rolling stock, the Cornwall Railway never had any locomotives of its own. It relied on the South Devon Railway for these, as well as for drivers and firemen. The Cornwall Railway was finally amalgamated with the Great Western on 1 July 1889.

The Liskeard & Caradon Railway

The Liskeard & Caradon Railway was incorporated on 27 June 1843 and, as a standard gauge line built on granite blocks, was opened from Moorswater at Liskeard northwards to South Caradon on 28 November 1844. By March 1846 a branch was opened from Caradon to Cheesewring, via a short inclined plane at Gonamena. The railway connected at Moorswater with the terminus of the Liskeard & Looe Union Canal, whence the copper from the rich South and West Caradon Mines, and granite from the Cheesewring and other quarries, were conveyed by barges to Looe. The canal had opened in 1828 and in its early years the ore and granite were brought down to Moorswater by carts. The railway was operated by detached wagons coming down from the mines and quarries, controlled by brakesmen, the wagons being hauled back by horses the following day. These horses were stabled by the Company at Moorswater. Although passenger traffic was not sanctioned by the Board of Trade, passengers were conveyed in wagons unofficially and at their own risk by obtaining a 'free pass', issued if a fare was paid for a hat, umbrella or parcel! Passenger accommodation was provided from 1860 and Sunday School outings to Cheesewring were popular.

The canal proved inadequate for the heavy traffic and so the Canal Company constructed a railway, mostly built on the canal banks. As the Liskeard & Looe Railway, this was opened on 27 December 1860 from Moorswater where there was an end-on junction, to Looe quay. Thus Looe was connected with Caradon and Cheesewring. By 1862 the Looe line was worked by the Liskeard & Caradon Company, who rebuilt their own line to accommodate locomotives, and extended it to Tokenbury Corner.

Twenty years later the line was further extended from Tokenbury around the eastern side of Caradon Hill to Cheesewring and Minions, connecting with the Kilmar Granite Tramway. The more direct incline section via Gonamena was then closed. There were goods depots at Polwrath, East Caradon, Tokenbury and Minions, with the engine and wagon sheds and ancillary buildings at Moorswater. An extension was proposed from a point near Kilmar northwards across Bodmin Moor to connect with Launceston. Some bridges were built, granite sleepers

2-4-0 T Lady Margaret *seen in the early 1900s at Looe, where pilchard barrels were often stacked on the platform*

were laid and the line completed to formation level for some distance but it was later abandoned. Had it materialised, there might possibly have been a passenger service from Launceston to Looe.

Meanwhile on 11 September 1879 passenger services commenced between Moorswater and Looe. A traveller from the main line at Liskeard, then unconnected, would find some difficulty in locating Moorswater station in the valley below Moorswater viaduct. The station consisted of a short platform of granite blocks, on which was a wooden building with a galvanised roof, divided into a booking office and a waiting room. Lavatory accommodation and a small goods shed were adjacent. The coaches, painted a dark reddish-brown, were either composite (first, second and third) or third class, but only the first and second class were upholstered. Oil lamps provided a very poor light. Buildings at the intermediate stops at Causeland and Sandplace consisted of sleeper huts. Sandplace appears to have been more important as it had a door – indeed it then had a siding where goods and coal traffic were handled, and it was not uncommon for the train to collect wagons

The Liskeard-Looe line is one of the great delights of the Cornish rail network. Scenically wonderful, it has the atmosphere of a Victorian branch line, with request stops and a reversal at the foot of the steep incline from Liskeard. Park-and-ride facilities at Liskeard make it the ideal way to approach Looe

there and proceed to Looe with wagons in front of and at the rear of the engine. Looe station was similar in appearance to Moorswater, and beyond this point the line then continued to Looe quay. Barrels of pilchards were a not unusual consignment at Looe. The first locomotive to work the Liskeard & Caradon was *Caradon*, built in 1862. In the twelve months following its introduction, traffic in ore, coal and granite exceeded 63,000 tons and an additional engine, *Cheesewring*, was acquired in 1864, followed by a third, *Kilmar* in 1869. These had no cabs, merely a flat weather-board with two 'portholes' in it, but in bad weather a canopy was erected to afford some protection.

A notable derailment happened at Tremar Coombe with *Kilmar* hauling a load of granite blocks. With the engine over the crossing, the rail stone blocks moved outwards, due to heavy rain, and several wagons went down between them. *Kilmar* was able to return next day with a

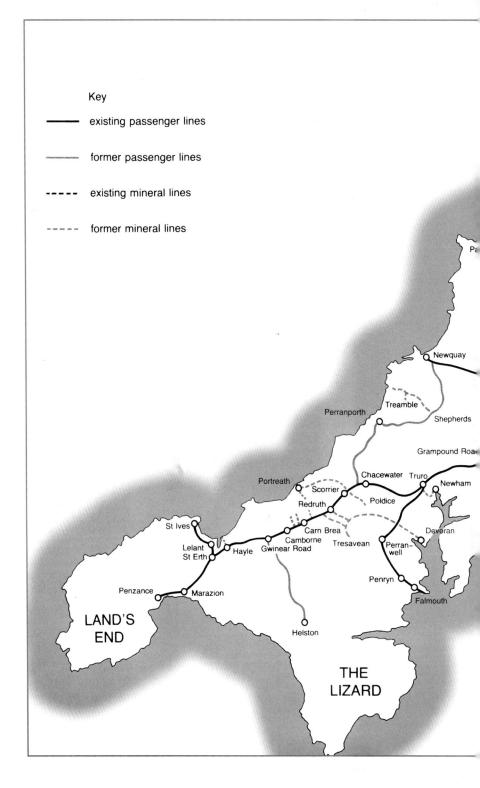

Key

— existing passenger lines

— former passenger lines

- - - - existing mineral lines

- - - - former mineral lines

Pa

Newquay

Treamble

Perranporth

Shepherds

Grampound Roa

Chacewater   Truro

Portreath   Scorrier   Newham

Redruth   Poldice

Carn Brea   Devoran

St Ives   Camborne   Tresavean

Lelant   Gwinear Road   Perran-

St Erth   Hayle   well

Penryn

Penzance   Marazion   Falmouth

LAND'S
END   Helston

THE
LIZARD

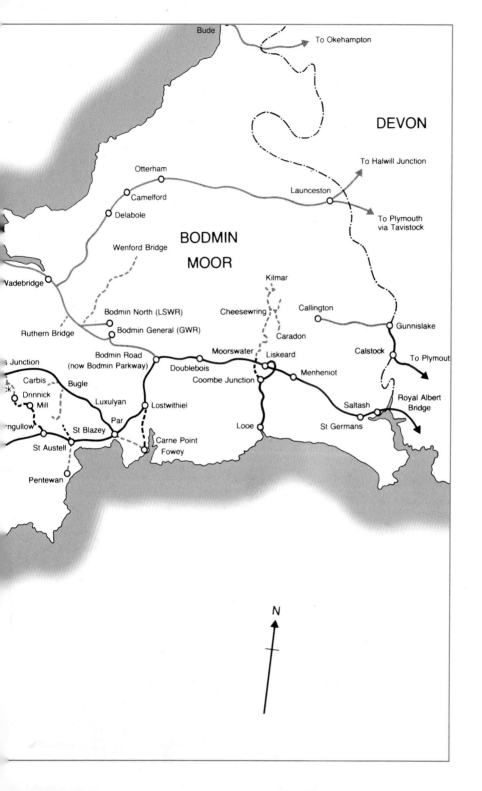

gang and lifting tackle. Of later engines, the 2-4-0 tank engine, *Lady Margaret*, usually undertook the working of the Looe line. Built in 1902, it survived on the GWR until 1948.

In 1901, the Liskeard & Looe opened a connecting loop line from Coombe Junction near Moorswater to Liskeard, where there was a new platform at right angles to the main line. The Looe company's goods yard at Liskeard was second in size in the county only to Truro. Trains descended from Liskeard by steep gradients, dropping some 150 ft to Coombe where the Looe trains had to reverse. It was said that if one missed the train for Looe at Liskeard, it was possible to hare down Lodge Hill and catch it at Coombe! With the opening of the latter station, passenger service at Moorswater was discontinued. A halt had also been opened at St Keyne, midway to Looe.

The GWR worked both the Liskeard & Looe and the Liskeard & Caradon lines from 1 January 1909 and acquired the latter in the same year. The Liskeard & Looe was not absorbed until the grouping in 1923. With the closing of the last of the Caradon mines and decline in traffic, all lines north of Moorswater were abandoned on 31 December 1916 and the rails dismantled soon after.

Sandplace Halt about 1970

THE CORNWALL MINERALS RAILWAY

The Cornwall Minerals Railway system resulted from a number of lines built by J T Treffry of Fowey, an enterprising and wealthy landowner with considerable interests in several lucrative local mines. He set about linking the north and south coasts of the county and first built a tram-road from the quarry at Colcerrow, to the east of Luxulyan, to convey stone to be used in constructing a viaduct across the valley.

By 1847 he had completed a canal from Par to Ponts Mill and a standard gauge tramroad known as the Par Railway, from Ponts Mill to Molinnis near Bugle. In 1855 the line was extended beside the canal to Par Harbour. This served the granite quarries and the eastern edge of the important china clay district. The tramroad ascended the side of Luxulyan valley by an inclined plane 947 yards long, known as Carmears Incline, which was rope-worked by a water-wheel. The line, worked by horses, then crossed the valley by the magnificent granite Treffry Viaduct, 216 yards long and 98 feet high, which also served as an aqueduct. A branch to Colcerrow was in operation from 1841, before the main line, to convey the granite for the viaduct.

By 1849 Treffry had opened the Newquay Railway from Newquay harbour to St Dennis, with a branch to the lead mine East Wheal Rose. The line ascended from the harbour by a cable-worked incline through a tunnel, and crossed Trenance Valley by a viaduct. Built on stone piers, its wooden superstructure was replaced by girders in 1874.

Treffry, who had become Chairman of the Cornwall Railway, died in 1850 and it was not until 21 July 1873 that the Cornwall Minerals Railway was incorporated, to take over Treffry's railways and build various new lines, all of which were to accommodate locomotives. By 1 June 1874 a single line from Fowey to Newquay was opened to goods. The line included Treffry's Par Railway to Bugle, and Newquay Railway to St Dennis, but a new section was built in the Luxulyan Valley under the Treffry Viaduct, replacing Carmears Incline, and another deviation between St Dennis Junction and Halloon avoided Toldish Tunnel. The viaduct remains to this day as a lasting tribute to the pioneering work of Treffry. In reaching Fowey the Company had to construct what was the longest tunnel in the county, that at St Pinnock, 1173 yards long.

Other lines opened on the same day by the Cornwall Minerals

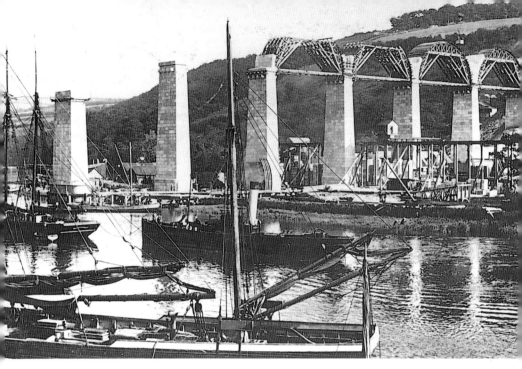

Calstock Viaduct under construction across the Tamar, 18 July 1906

Railway were the Carbis branch from Bugle to Carbis, the Retew branch from St Dennis Junction to Melangoose Mill, that from Tolcarn Junction past East Wheal Rose and Treamble to Gravel Hill, and Bodmin Road (later St Dennis Junction) to Drinnick Mill.

Meanwhile, in 1869, the Newquay & Cornwall Junction Railway had been opened from Burngullow to Drinnick Mill; this too was taken over and operated by the Cornwall Minerals Railway in 1874. The section from Burngullow to Drinnick Mill was laid as broad gauge and the remainder as standard instead of mixed gauge as authorised. Pressure from the Cornwall Railway led to a third, broad gauge, rail being laid, but in such an indifferent way that it was never used and there was the anomaly of break of gauge at Drinnick Mill until the end of broad gauge in 1892. Between 1909 and 1922, through traffic from Burngullow to St Dennis was temporarily halted, due to the Carpella United Clay Company having the right to excavate under the track.

This important mineral line serving the heart of the china clay area has never carried passengers and although Drinnick Mill has no proper station, it was important enough to have a station master.

On 20 June 1876 a passenger service was introduced between Fowey and Newquay, with intermediate stops at Par, St Blazey, Bridges for Luxulyan, Bugle, Victoria for Roche (previously Holywell) and Halloon. There were several changes in name. Par became St Blazey on the opening of the Par-St Blazey loop in 1879. Halloon became St Columb Road and in GWR ownership Victoria was changed to Roche, and Bridges to Luxulyan.

The Lostwithiel & Fowey Railway opened a broad gauge line for clay from Lostwithiel to Carne Point in June 1869. It was worked by the Cornwall Railway but was forced to close in 1880. It was transferred to the Cornwall Minerals Railway in 1892 and reopened and extended to Fowey on 16 September 1895.

The GWR worked the 47 miles of line owned by this Company from October 1877 onwards. The only exception was the Goonbarrow clay works branch from Bugle, which the Company itself worked. The Cornwall Minerals Railway lost its identity on 1 July 1896 on absorption by the GWR.

THE TAMAR, KIT HILL & CALLINGTON RAILWAY

In 1864 part of this line was laid as the Tamar, Kit Hill & Callington Railway, but it was as the East Cornwall Mineral Railway that it was opened on 7 May 1872. It was intended to serve the mines around Gunnislake, Stoke Climsland and Kelly Bray, as well as the quarries on Kit Hill. Of 3 ft 6 in gauge, it rose from sidings on Calstock quay beside the Tamar by a single track rope-worked incline nearly 800 feet in length. From here locomotives operated the seven miles to Kelly Bray which lies one mile from Callington. Shunting on Calstock quay was performed by horses. There were several sidings serving the tin, copper and arsenic mines and the quarries. Gunnislake Clitters Mine and Kit Hill Quarries were connected by inclined tramways. Public depots were situated at Drakewalls, Cox's Park, Monks Corner and Kelly Bray.

In 1891 the Plymouth, Devonport & South Western Junction Railway took the line over. It was converted to standard gauge and a connecting link constructed from its own line at Bere Alston, across the stone viaduct at Calstock to join the old East Cornwall Mineral line south of Gunnislake. With the construction of the new line, part of the former ECMR, including the incline, was abandoned. Calstock Viaduct had twelve arches each spanning 60 feet and rose 120 feet above the river. To provide access from the viaduct to the quay below, a wagon lift was built with a capacity of one open wagon fully loaded, to a maximum of 20 tons. The lift survived until 1934, when with the decline of barge traffic on the river, it was dismantled and sold. On 2 March 1908 the new line was opened with stations at Calstock, Gunnislake (formerly Drakewalls depot), Latchley (Cox's Park), Stoke Climsland (Monk's Corner) and Callington Road (Kelly Bray). So many people travelled on the opening day that no less than £100 was received in fares.

For the newly opened line, three engines were built, a pair of 0-6-2T named *Earl of Mount Edgcumbe* and *Lord St Levan* (after two directors) and an 0-6-0T named *A S Harris* (after the first secretary of the Company). The following year Stoke Climsland was renamed Luckett; in its early days it had a station-mistress, probably the first in Britain. A halt was opened at Chilsworthy and another was provided at Seven Stones in 1910. It became popular for Plymouth people coming to picnic at the nearby Phoenix Pleasure grounds and survived until their closure in September 1917.

In later years the locomotive used became affectionately known as 'The Kelly Bray Express' or 'Whistler', due to its noisy approach to a number of occupational crossings. The line remained in the control of the PD&SWJR until the grouping of 1923 when it passed to the ownership of the Southern Railway.

THE LONDON & SOUTH WESTERN RAILWAY

The London & South Western Railway had acquired the Bodmin & Wadebridge Railway in 1846, but it was to be some years before they were able to reach it from their own system. The Launceston & South Devon Railway opened its broad gauge line for passengers to Launceston on 1 July 1865, extended from Tavistock and Lydford. Relations between the SDR and the GWR on the one side and the LSWR on the other were never very happy, and keen rivalry existed.

It was not until July 1886 that the North Cornwall Railway, incorporated on 18 August 1882, reached Launceston from Halwill Junction. The North Cornwall was to be worked by the LSWR, and its station at Launceston adjoined that of the rival Launceston & South Devon. In its

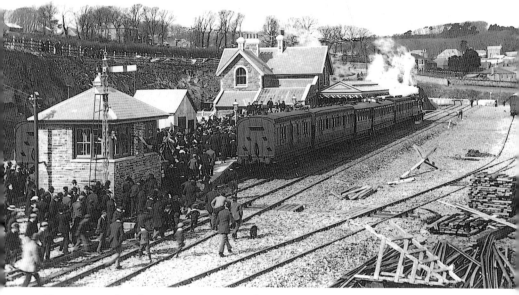

The opening of Padstow Station, 27 March 1899

prospectus for the remainder of the proposed line from Launceston to Wadebridge and Padstow, the directors of the North Cornwall Railway stated that with the guarantees of the LSWR and having regard to the general conditions of the Railway, they had no hesitation in submitting the undertaking as a safe and desirable investment. The extension of the LSWR system would open up an entirely new district, 400 square miles in extent, to railway communication on an unbroken gauge from all parts of England, and be worked, stocked and maintained by the LSWR. It was estimated that a minimum annual traffic of 25,000 tons would be forthcoming from the Old Delabole Slate Company. It was emphasised that only a 24 mile extension was needed from Wadebridge to Truro to make it a main line to Penzance and Falmouth from London and the North.

The optimism of those early days was somewhat tempered by the very slow progress, caused by lack of funds, in building the line across the open North Cornish countryside. After reaching Launceston in 1886, it was not until July 1892 that the section from Launceston to Tresmeer was opened. Tresmeer to Camelford was opened in August

1893, Camelford to Delabole in October 1893 and Delabole to Wade-bridge in June 1895. Thus the LSWR at last reached its own Bodmin & Wadebridge line. Stations were also situated at Otterham, Port Isaac Road and St Kew Highway, plus Egloskerry in November 1892. Wadebridge station, already rebuilt, had an island platform added to accommodate North Cornwall traffic. Although the track was single, passing loops were provided at all intermediate stations. The population was sparse in the area traversed by the railway, but tourists were now more readily able to reach coastal beauty spots such as Crackington Haven, Boscastle, Tintagel, Port Isaac and Polzeath.

A few years later, in August 1898, the LSWR completed its line from Okehampton via Halwill Junction to Holsworthy by extending it to Bude. It was nearly twenty years after opening to Holsworthy that the railway eventually reached Bude, which would no doubt have developed more rapidly as a resort had the delay not been so protracted. Bude consisted of one main and one bay platform, with the line continuing to the canal wharf. It could boast of a busy engine shed.

The North Cornwall Railway's last addition was opened on 27 March 1899 with the section from Wadebridge along the picturesque Camel estuary to Padstow. Before constructing this extension a Board of Trade enquiry was held concerning the proposal to use the route over Wadebridge level crossing, then only used infrequently for traffic to the quay. Although not acted upon, it recommended a deviation, one reason being the large amount of vehicular and foot traffic passing over it – amounting on market days to an average of 45 vehicles, 7 horses, 35 cattle and 476 foot passengers per hour. One witness, contemplating an eventual through line from Launceston to Truro, considered it a danger even in its existing form as he had lost a horse in consequence of its being frightened by a train.

Approaching Padstow, the line crossed Little Petherick Creek by the Iron Bridge, before running into the station, 260 miles from Waterloo. The layout included a turntable and lengthy sidings running down to the quay. In Southern days a new ocean fish terminal was built, opposite the passenger platform, the up train to Exeter which conveyed the fish being affectionately known as 'the Perisher'. Passenger services from Waterloo always contained through coaches to Padstow, but with the introduction in 1947 of 4-6-2 Bulleid 'West Country' engines, light

32

enough in axle loading to work the branch, long trains reached the far terminus. The Atlantic Coast Express became a familiar sight, particularly during the holiday season, and the turntable at Padstow had to be replaced by a new one of 70 ft to accommodate the new locomotives.

General passenger traffic on the rest of the North Cornwall was always light, except on summer Saturdays when trains were well filled with holidaymakers. In addition the line handled fair quantities of slate and agricultural produce. The two lengthy sections from Okehampton to Bude and from Halwill to Wadebridge and Padstow were later to become known as part of the Southern Railway's 'withered arm', the nickname given to its sprawling system in North Devon and Cornwall.

THE GREAT WESTERN RAILWAY

By the turn of the century the GWR had acquired the West Cornwall Railway, the Cornwall Railway and the Cornwall Minerals Railway, and had constructed its own branches to St Ives and Bodmin. It was later to take over the Liskeard & Caradon and Liskeard & Looe lines. One other railway to be absorbed was the Helston line, incorporated by the Helston Railway Act of 9 July 1880. Schemes to connect Helston with Penryn had been promoted as early as 1846, the time of the Railway Mania, so named because of the boom in promoting new railways, but when the line was opened on 9 May 1887, it was from Gwinear Road on the main line. It was worked from the outset by the GWR and vested in them from 1 July 1898. Various setbacks had delayed its construction since the first sod was cut in 1882. The customary festivities marked the opening and in Helston street collections raised £150 towards the cost of celebrations, and public meetings appointed committees to superintend the decorations, free tea and firework display. Huge floral arches were erected with such slogans as 'Success to the Helston Railway', 'One and All', 'Union is Strength', 'Prosperity to the Trade of Helston', 'Fish, Tin and Copper', 'Welcome'.

Intermediate stations were situated at Praze and Nancegollan, whence the line continued to Cober Viaduct and on to Helston, where there were both locomotive and carriage sheds. The line continued for a distance beyond the platform, with the original intention of extending it to the Lizard. This was not to be, although in 1903 the GWR introduced its first omnibus service from Helston to Mullion and the Lizard,

Horse buses, later replaced by motor buses owned by the GWR, took passengers from Helston to Mullion and Lizard Town

and followed this in later years by other services in the area.

In 1905 Truthall Halt was opened and in constructing this isolated platform some lengths of the old Barlow rail, replaced on the main line, were used. Nancegollan station was rebuilt in 1937 and a passing loop provided, the only one on the branch. As with most other Cornish lines, passenger traffic was heavy only in the summer season, whilst freight mostly comprised agricultural produce.

The broad gauge, which had survived on the lines of the South Devon and Cornwall Railways, came to an end on 20 May 1892, when all obsolete rolling stock had to be worked back east of Exeter. This displaced stock covered 15 miles of siding. The mammoth task of converting the line between Exeter and Truro, together with certain branches, was exceptionally well organised and completed in two days. Something like 5000 men took part, deployed at about 25 per mile of track.

The next ten years saw lines doubled and bridges strengthened or rebuilt. By 1908 the main line had been doubled from St Germans westward to Truro and the newly rebuilt Truro Viaduct was in use. Between Saltash and St Germans part of the existing line was replaced by a four mile deviation inland, completed by 1908. Of double track, this involved three new viaducts and a tunnel, but avoided five old timber viaducts. The last section of main line to be doubled was that between Scorrier and Drump Lane (Redruth), which was not completed until 1930. This left single track only over the Royal Albert Bridge.

The Chacewater to Newquay line was the next to be built, opened from Chacewater via Blackwater (where there was an east and a west facing junction to the main line), to Perranporth in July 1903, with new stations there and at St Agnes. In 1905 the line was extended from Perranporth to Shepherds station, where it connected with the mineral line from Tolcarn Junction to Treamble, thus enabling trains to run through to Newquay. Later that year halts were opened on this line at Mount Hawke, Goonbell, Mithian, Goonhavern, Mitchell & Newlyn and Trewerry & Trerice. A further halt at Perranporth Beach was not built until 1931. Blackwater Junction was removed in 1924 and the branch line continued independently, for ease of working, through to Chacewater. Of the remainder of the Treamble branch, not incorporated in the passenger line, that from Treamble to Gravel Hill was closed in 1888 and the track removed. The remaining section from

Converting the last of the broad gauge, Forder near Saltash, May 1892

Par Station in the early 1900s – tricky weather conditions but nothing the GWR couldn't handle

Shepherds to Treamble was closed in 1917, but re-opened in 1926 with a mining revival. It was last used in 1949 and closed by 1952. On the Par-Newquay line, Quintrell Downs Platform came into use in 1911. The following year the Retew clay branch from St Dennis Junction to Melangoose Mill was extended to Meledor Mill. In 1920 the Trenance Valley clay line opened from Trenance Junction near St Austell first to Bojea and then to Lansalson. 1926 saw the closure of the line from Newquay harbour to the station, but in later years the station itself was extended.

On the main line, Burngullow station was rebuilt on a new site in 1901 and finally disappeared from the passenger timetable in 1931. Two main line halts were opened in 1905, at Copperhouse near Hayle and at Dolcoath, which were in use until 1908. Near Saltash, Defiance Platform was introduced in 1905 and continued until 1930. Probus & Ladock Halt, between Truro and Grampound Road, was built in 1908.

On 1 July 1904 the first Cornish Riviera Express was run, requiring extensions to platforms at most intermediate stations. Before that date the journey from Paddington to Penzance had taken 8½ hours: with its introduction, the time was reduced to 7 hours. It was then called the Limited Express, and to railwaymen has always been known as the

'Limited'. For many years it was hauled by the great Churchward 'Star' class engines, followed in the 1920s by the equally famous Collett 'Castles' and 'Kings'. West of Plymouth the first trains were headed by 4-4-0 engines of the 'Bulldog' class, whose smaller driving wheels were considered an advantage on the Cornish banks. The run from Paddington as far as Plymouth remained for years the longest and fastest non-stop journey on the Great Western. Departure times were traditionally 10.30 am from Paddington and 10 am from Penzance, and as far back as 1927 the '10.30 Limited' had to be run in four parts at busy summer weekends. Steam gave way in 1958 to the 'Warship' class diesels. The journey from Paddington to Penzance is now completed in five hours exactly.

At Fowey at the beginning of the century the railway quays were developed considerably, to deal with increasing quantities of china clay for export by sea. At this time Fowey was blessed with two passenger services, but the one from St Blazey via Pinnock Tunnel was closed to passengers on 8 July 1929, though trains for workmen were still run until the end of 1934. Station improvements continued over the years, the main rebuilding being that of the main line terminus at Penzance in 1937. At the same period considerable additional sidings were provided between there and Marazion, to cope with the storage of passenger and mail coaches and handle agricultural produce and fish from Newlyn.

NATIONALISATION

As a result of the 1947 Transport Act, which nationalised Britain's railways, control of the former GWR lines and stations passed to the Western Region's Plymouth District, and Southern lines and stations passed to the Southern Region's Exeter District. Otherwise, things carried on much as before. Indeed in 1948 the restaurant car on the Atlantic Coast Express went all the way to Padstow.

However, there were a few minor changes. For example, in 1949 the two stations in Bodmin town were renamed to avoid confusion, the former GWR station becoming Bodmin General and the Southern, Bodmin North. Also around this time the Western were allowed to run a couple of through trains to Padstow, and the Southern train was diverted from Bodmin North on its last working of the day to serve Bodmin Road.

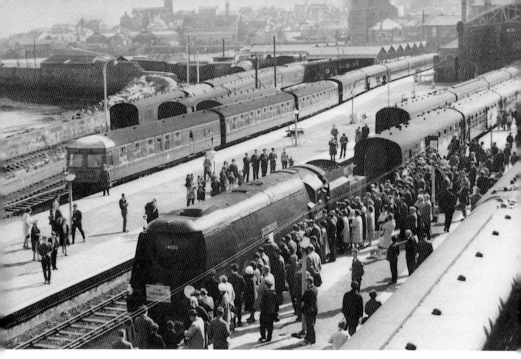

The last British Railways steam train at Penzance , and the first ex-Southern Region 'West Country' Class to visit the town, 3 May 1964

In Launceston, where the two railways had lived side by side and ignored each other (save for a common signal box installed in 1915), the stations became North and South on 18 June 1951. It was also in Launceston just one year later that the first economy was made: from 30 June 1952 the former GWR North station was closed to passengers and services were diverted to South station. This was made possible by utilising the 1943 wartime emergency junction.

The only other changes of note in the 1950s were the transfer in 1952 of all Southern region stations to the Western region for commercial purposes – i.e. ticket sales and promotional material. The Southern continued to be responsible for running the trains; full control was returned to the Southern in 1958. On the Western main line the Probus & Ladock platform closed on 2 December 1957, myxomatosis having killed off the lucrative rabbit trade in the area.

As 1960 dawned, a decade of great change lay on the horizon. As well as the effects of car ownership and an increase in commercial lorries making inroads into both passenger and freight revenues, diesel was about to have a huge impact on the railways.

The first diesel-hauled train had been seen in 1958 when Cornwall (and most of Devon) was earmarked as one of the first areas in the country to be dieselised. In 1961 steam was still common in Cornwall. By 1962 it still reigned supreme on the former Southern lines, but was becoming a rare sight on the Western lines where by the middle of 1963 it had gone completely. The last British Rail steam train from Plymouth to Penzance ran on 3 May 1964. Early the next year, when the Bude and North Cornwall lines were dieselised on 4 January 1965, the age of steam was but a memory.

The 1960s also saw the run down and closure of many stations and lines – Carn Brea on the main line was the first to go, in 1961. Branch line closures then began in 1962 with Gwinear Road to Helston losing its passenger service on 5 November. The GWR route from Plymouth to Launceston closed in a blizzard as 1962 ended and 1963 began, at which point all former Southern lines in Cornwall (and everywhere else west of Wilton South, near Salisbury) were transferred to the Western Region. Chacewater-Newquay shut completely from 4 February the same year, except for Tolcarn Junction to Trevemper Siding which survived for freight until the October.

Apart from advocating a few reprieves (the Looe, St Ives and Gunnislake lines, together with the intermediate stations between Par and Newquay), the Beeching Report of March 1963 was as ruthless in its implications for Cornwall as elsewhere. It proposed closure of the following lines: Bere Alston-Callington, Bodmin Road/Bodmin North-Wadebridge-Padstow, Liskeard-Looe, Lostwithiel-Fowey, Okehampton-Bude and Wadebridge, and St Erth-St Ives.

Amid the flurry of closures came, somewhat surprisingly, the construction of Boscarne Exchange Platform which was opened in June 1964 just as steam to Bodmin North finished. A new diesel railbus was then introduced from the Exchange Platform to Bodmin North, connecting out of the Bodmin Road-Padstow diesel railcar service. But the Exchange proved to be one of Cornwall's shortest lived stations and was shut in January 1967 when the whole system lost its passenger service.

In the first weekend of September 1964 momentous changes took place: on the 5th, the Bulleid Pacific engine *Exmouth* brought the Atlantic Coast Express into Padstow for the last time. From the 7th, through services between Waterloo and Bude and Padstow were withdrawn. And on the same day the GWR route from Lifton to Launceston was reopened to allow the withdrawal of freight on the North Cornwall route. Bere Alston-Callington was also dieselised – no more the bark of an Ivatt tank as it climbed high through the Tamar valley.

A month later on 5 October, six Western main line stations passed from the passenger timetable: Doublebois, Grampound Road, Chacewater, Scorrier, Gwinear Road and Marazion. In addition, the Helston branch closed completely. The next year Lostwithiel-Fowey closed quietly to passengers from 4 January. Less quiet was the abandonment of Okehampton-Bude and Halwill-Wadebridge on 3 October 1966. Large crowds assembled, especially at Bude and Launceston, for the last trains. The single diesel railcar from Wadebridge was so packed that children rode on the luggage racks. A second car was added at Launceston, and at Halwill these were joined by two more from Bude. It is worth reflecting that the GWR route to Launceston had closed to goods (for the second time) from 28 February 1966, and the demise of the North Cornwall system removed a large slice from the railway map.

From 7 November 1966 Gunnislake-Callington was shut to passengers, freight having already succumbed earlier in the year, although the wonderful stretch from Gunnislake to Bere Alston, including Calstock Viaduct, was retained due to the difficult terrain for alternative transport. A few months later the oldest passenger railway in the West Country, from Bodmin North to Wadebridge, closed on 30 January 1967 with the withdrawal of the Bodmin Road-Padstow passenger service.

Nor did the China Clay Mineral Lines escape the knife. The Wheal Rose Branch near Bugle, for example, had gone by 1964, Parkandillack-St Dennis Junction closed in 1966, and the Trenance Valley near St Austell had disappeared by May 1968. The Goonbarrow Branch from Goonbarrow Junction (on the Par-Newquay line), with a spectacular incline reversal at Gunheath and the 341 yard Stenalees tunnel, was also closed in 1965 beyond New Caudeldown. The line was cut back further in 1978 to leave only a few hundred yards as a headshunt for Rocks Dryers Sidings in Bugle which today still despatches substantial amounts of china clay to Fowey. The Retew branch to Meledor saw its last train in 1981.

As the china clay traffic continued to grow, the clay company desired road access to Fowey, where the harbour is capable of accommodating

Falmouth Docks in 1986, with the last regular working steam locomotive in Cornwall plying the quays

trans-Atlantic vessels. A pact was made to guarantee conveyance of clay by rail, both long haul (to the Potteries) and via Lostwithiel to Carne Point, in exchange for the Fowey-St Blazey line being closed from 1 July 1968 (it was immediately turned into a private road) and leased to the clay company for 200 years.

Other notable events during the 1960s include the opening in 1961 of the Tamar Road Bridge, built alongside Brunel's masterpiece. This led to an inevitable, but surprisingly not immediate, reduction in suburban traffic – Plymouth-Saltash local workings survived until May 1972. In May 1964 the line was singled over St Pinnock and Largin Viaducts to reduce maintenance costs and prolong the life of the structures. The track was realigned for higher speed, as was the case elsewhere for, as 1970 approached, the summer timetable for the first time allowed passengers to travel from Paddington to Penzance and back in a single day.

The blue and grey diesel and much rationalised railway of 1970 was in stark contrast to the chocolate and cream and green liveries of the great steam era from only a decade earlier. In fact, such was the carnage that for passengers just two former Southern stations, Calstock and

Gunnislake, remained open, while for freight only lines to Wadebridge and Wenford Bridge were in use. Eventually, however, even freight to Wadebridge ceased in September 1978, the line from Boscarne Junction closing officially at the start of 1979 after a series of special farewell trains. The freight-only Penwithers Junction-Newham line, a remnant of the original West Cornwall Railway, closed on 6 November 1971.

Falmouth, on the other hand, gained a new station (the structure was actually the re-sited Perranporth Beach Halt) at The Dell on 7 December 1970, but this was at the expense of the earlier terminus. Because of the gradient, the diesel multiple units had to continue empty to the old terminus, which was reopened as Falmouth Docks in May 1975. The Dell was retained and is now known as Falmouth Town.

On the main line the emphasis was very much on improving the Inter-City Service. The summer timetable of May 1972, for instance, saw the renamed 'Cornish Riviera Limited' reaching Penzance in 5 hours and 23 minutes from London – only 23 minutes behind the very fast 'Cornishman' which left Bradford at 07.00. The 'Golden Hind' had by then been extended to and from Penzance, allowing 6 hours in the capital on day trips. This would have been unthinkable in steam days.

Another positive step forward came when Multiple Aspect Signalling was brought to Cornwall in July 1973 and the Plymouth Panel Signal Box was extended to a new boundary at St Germans. (A further extension on 27 April 1998 saw Liskeard become the new boundary for traditional signalling.) In May 1978 Lelant Saltings was opened to provide a park and ride facility for St Ives and has since proved very successful.

The 1980s began with the introduction of the full high speed train service to London. In May 1980 the 'Golden Hind' took a mere 5 hours for the 305 1/4 mile journey to London. Today the trains are serviced at Long Rock depot, whose construction in the late 1970s coincided with the singling of the line from Marazion to Penzance. It is owned by First Great Western. Virgin Trains berth a couple of trains from Glasgow overnight.

The Hayle Wharves freight line finished in 1982, but on 12 July 1983 Bodmin Road became Bodmin Parkway to herald the arrival of 'Cornish Railways'. With headquarters at Truro, local management were given semi-independence and they co-ordinated all activities. The 'Cornish Lizard' even appeared on some rolling stock.

The Launceston Steam Railway in 1991, a narrow gauge line running on the original trackbed, run by steam preservation enthusiasts

Business and morale rose, and the Cornish railcard was introduced. It was the first railcard in Britain available to everyone, giving discounts on virtually all travel west of Plymouth (it is still actively marketed by the train operating companies today). But independence lasted a mere three years until May 1986, after which the Plymouth Area Manager took over. In turn, unified control was gradually broken up as the BR business sectors rose to prominence.

Conveyance of china clay from Wenford Bridge to the main line at Bodmin Parkway, involving reversals at Boscarne Junction and Bodmin General, survived until 1983 when the whole system closed on 18 November. This brought to an end the last portion in use of the Bodmin & Wadebridge Railway of 1834. A successful preservation society was formed the following year – see page 46.

Meanwhile, preservation activity was starting at the other end of the county. On Boxing Day 1983 the narrow gauge Launceston Steam Railway commenced operations. The 1 ft 11 1/2 in gauge line has its base just west of the original station, and is built on the LSWR North Cornwall trackbed, running through the delightful scenery of the Kensey valley. Progressive extensions have been made, the last opening to New Mills in May 1995.

Truro Station in 1971, before track and signalling alterations

Industrial steam in Cornwall continued beyond the BR steam era. It was originally introduced to the Par Harbour System in 1912 and lasted until 1977, but Falmouth Docks had an even longer association: steam was brought in when the first ship dry-docked in 1861. Locomotive number 3, the last steam locomotive in regular use in Cornwall, retired on 23 August 1986. It was subsequently sold into preservation on the Plym Valley Railway in Plymouth where it powered the first public passenger train on 14 October 2001.

An unexpected move was the singling of the main line to Probus on 5 October 1986, the net result being the creation of an unnecessary bottle-neck. Burngullow signal box was abolished and the area was controlled from a mini-panel in Par signal box.

Around about this time the chocolate and cream 'Skipper' trains – bus bodies on a four-wheel chassis – were introduced. Unfortunately they proved allergic to the Gunnislake, Looe and St Ives lines, and were hastily replaced by hurriedly imported first generation DMUs. These lasted until March 1997 when Sprinter domination became complete.

Like all other lines in Cornwall, the Par-Newquay branch contracted in the 1960s, and yet right up until the end of the 1987 season diesels brought up to 14 coaches on summer Saturdays to the county's longest platforms. Capacity was somewhat reduced in 1986 by abolition of the loop at St Dennis and in October the following year by closure of Newquay signal box. High speed trains coming from London, Leeds and Edinburgh took over at the start of the 1988 season, and today on summer Saturdays can deliver over 2000 people to the Atlantic coast at Newquay. With such limited capacity, overcrowding and minimal service remain a problem.

On the freight side, the internal transport in Cornwall of china clay to the docks at Fowey eventually had to be looked at very carefully. This was largely because the traffic was (and still is) heavy, and the ageing clay hood wagons ultimately became redundant. A fifteen-year contract with BR to handle the business came into effect on 1 October 1987, and involved a large investment of £4 million to purchase a fleet of 124 new large capacity CDA wagons. At the time of writing the present operators are seeking economies to maintain the traffic.

A stunning photograph of Calstock Viaduct in 2001. The Gunnislake branch is another delightful survival

A Virgin Cross-Country diesel crossing Forder Viaduct, 2001

PRIVATISATION AND PRESERVATION

And so to the 1990s, the decade dominated by the break up of the national system into far too many parts and its passage into private hands, although it was not all doom and gloom: the Bodmin & Wenford Railway reopened the line from Bodmin General to Bodmin Parkway on 17 June 1990, marking the welcome return of a steam branch line. Bodmin General-Boscarne Junction (where a brand new station was built) was also reopened, on 15 August 1996. The B & W is a very friendly railway and, full of atmosphere, provides a perfect recreation of the steam age, as the photographs on the cover and page 9 show. A visit is thoroughly recommended.

The break up and sale of the national network, even as far as Cornwall is concerned, is far too long and complicated for this little book. Suffice to say that by the time the Western Region had passed into history in the early 1990s, the British Railways Board had created 'Business Sectors' which for Cornwall meant Inter-City, Provincial (later Regional Railways), Transrail and Rail Express Systems.

Railtrack took over ownership and operation of all railway infrastructure from 1 April 1994. At the same time the assets of Inter-City were separated into Great Western or Cross Country, the latter having separate offices at Plymouth – very different from the unified Cornish Railways of ten years earlier. The first privatised trains to run were the mail trains of Rail Express Systems. These were later taken over in December 1995 by the English, Welsh & Scottish Railway. Next were the London trains, sold to Great Western Trains on 4 February 1996. Ten days later Transrail's freight trains went to EWS.

EWS has established a solid base at St Blazey. It has invested heavily in new locomotives, including the American-built Class 66 which arrived in the county for the first time in January 1999, and the Spanish-built Class 67 which were introduced in Spring 2000 for the mail trains, giving Cornwall some of the newest locomotives in the country. As well as dominating the clay workings through its Internal China Clay to Fowey and trains to Cliff Vale, Stoke-on-Trent and Irvine, Scotland, EWS brings cement from Earls Sidings, Hope, in the Peak District, to Moorswater and occasionally coal to Falmouth.

On 13 October 1996 Wales & West took Regional Railways Services (i.e. all the branch lines except Newquay on summer Saturdays) and the mainline stoppers with their Manchester & Cardiff Sprinter workings. This left two cross-country trains to and from Scotland as the last BR-operated trains in Cornwall, but these passed to Virgin Cross Country early in 1997. Virgin have now added a Glasgow train to their other two Scottish Expresses but the return train goes only as far as Manchester.

Great Western – which became part of First Group in 1998 and consequently First Great Western – has its headquarters in Swindon, but it also has Long Rock depot and separate offices outside Penzance station. It has expanded its London services, which resulted in 1999 in the reappearance of some locomotive-hauled trains.

On 14 October 2001 Wales & West was disbanded into two franchises: Wales & Borders (an all-Welsh franchise, rather like the Cornish Railways of the 1980s, operating through services between Manchester/Cardiff and Penzance) and Wessex Trains (including local trains and lines in Devon and Cornwall). The contract with Wessex Trains, part of the National Express Group, is for a limited period, after which it may be awarded elsewhere.

Handling china clay by rail, today (above) and as it was done on the Pentewan Railway at St Austell in the nineteenth century

As this book goes to press there appears to be unprecedented passenger dissatisfaction with services to and within the south west, and improvements are eagerly awaited. But having said that, the privatised railway in Cornwall entering the twenty-first century is actually busier in passenger numbers than ever before, EWS has made efforts to regain freight (though with little success as yet), and the china clay business is brisk. It seems that, after all the turmoil in Cornwall's history of rail transport, we can in fact look forward to a reasonably healthy future.